Bible Story Puppets and Poems

by Sharon Thompson

illustrated by Vanessa Booth

It is the mission of Carson-Dellosa Christian Publishing to create the highest-quality Scripture-based children's products that teach the Word of God, share His love and goodness, assist in faith development, and glorify His Son, Jesus Christ.

"... teach me your ways so I may know you...."
Exodus 33:13

Credits
Editor: Erin Seltzer
Layout Design: Sharon Thompson
Cover Illustration: Dan Sharp
Cover Design: Peggy Jackson

Scripture taken from the HOLY BIBLE, NEW INTERNATIONAL VERSION Copyright © 1973, 1978, 1984 International Bible Society. Used by permission of Zondervan Bible Publishers.

ISBN: 1-59441-007-0

Contents

How to Use This Book

Bible Story Puppets and Poems teaches Bible stories through poetry. The plays engage children in three ways. Visual stimulation is provided through watching the finger puppet characters move. Auditory stimulation occurs while the poem is being read, and tactile stimulation comes into play when children maneuver the puppets themselves. In some poems, children are asked to participate by shouting, shaking fingers, or clapping.

These puppets and poems may be used over and over again. If you share a poem several times, children will eventually say it with you. The repetition will help children claim the messages of God's love and mercy as their own.

Sets and Scenery

All sets are designed to be copied, colored, cut out, and either glued or attached with removable adhesive to a shoebox or cardboard. You will need to look at the illustration of the set for each lesson since shoeboxes may be used and cut in different ways.

If you prefer a more permanent stage and have room to store various sets, you may prefer to glue scenery to the stages. Sets should be prepared outside of class time. You may wish to prepare them yourself or with help from older children. Some sets are used for more than one poem (such as the royal set that is used for both *Esther, Queen of Persia* and *David and Saul*).

The set for *Joseph and His Brothers* is attached to the bottom of a shoebox.

A box with an attached lid for storing the animals is best for *Noah Builds an Ark*.

The set for *Adam and Eve in the Garden* needs to have an arch cut from the bottom of a shoebox.

Puppets

Puppets should also be copied, colored, and cut out. Many puppets are finger puppets but some larger patterns need to be glued to craft sticks or the fingertips of gloves. Some puppets and crowd scenes may be attached directly to the scenery with removable adhesive. Removable adhesive will enable you to use the same puppets and sets again and again. In some cases, puppets are used for more than one poem. Directions on the pattern pages provide more specific instructions.

Questions and Lessons

When asking the questions, encourage students to share similar stories from their own life experiences. For example, after Adam and Eve ate from the Tree of Knowledge, they tried to hide from God. Ask children if they have ever done something their parents asked them not to do and tried to hide it.

The lessons are springboards for discussing the stories and how they relate to children's lives. Share the lessons in your own words and encourage students to share God's love.

In God's eyes,
his child Noah was good.
Among sinful men,
faithful Noah stood.

Noah appears.

God told Noah to
build a boat.
"I'm gonna flood the earth,
so the boat should float."

Noah looks up to the heavens.

Noah began to hammer
and he began to nail.
He followed God's instructions
to the very last detail.

Noah gets his hammer.
Noah hammers.

Noah got his sons
Japheth, Shem, and Ham.
"Go get your mother
and your wives—the rest of our fam."

They loaded up their family
and they didn't even mind
sharing the boat with animals,
two of every kind.

As the birds flew in the ark,
the ducks began to quack.
After all the birds were in,
came a great big hairy yak.

Doves, ravens, peacocks, toucans, and ostriches enter the ark.
Ducks enter the ark.

Yaks enter the ark.

In came lions and turtles,
giraffes, and even bears,
kangaroos, rhinos, and elephants.
They kept on coming in pairs.

Lions and turtles enter the ark.
Giraffes and bears enter the ark.
Kangaroos, rhinoceroses, and elephants enter the ark.
Deer, walruses, and iguanas enter the ark.

It began to rain,
and Noah finally shut the door.
His wife and family were on board
with animals galore!

Noah shuts the door.

For forty days and forty nights
the heavens brought forth rain.
It would be many days
before the waters began to wane.

Ark moves as if floating.

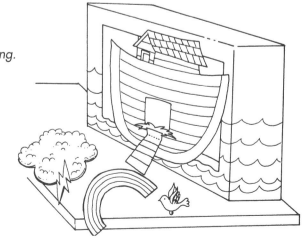

The waters went down
and the ark stopped floating and sat.
It landed atop a mountain
named Mount Ararat.

Water recedes.

Ark lands on the mountain.

First, Noah sent a raven
to look for land that was dry.
But going back and forth,
the raven continued to fly.

One raven exits the ark.

Raven flies.

Then, Noah sent a dove
to try to find dry land.
But when it could find none,
it flew back to Noah's hand.

One dove exits the ark.

Dove lands on Noah's hand.

The next time the dove returned
with an olive leaf in its beak.
The third time the dove kept flying.
No longer Noah did it seek.

Dove flies again.
Dove lands again.

Dove flies out of sight.

Then, God told Noah to come out
and bring his family.
He said, "Get out of that ark
and set those animals free."

Noah leaves the ark.
Noah's family leaves the ark.

Animals leave the ark and go to the foam core.

God promised never again
by a flood would everything die.
To mark His promise,
He placed a rainbow in the sky.

Rainbow appears close to the animals on foam core. See below.

Questions
1. Do you think people thought Noah was silly for building an ark when it wasn't even raining yet?
2. Do you think people laughed at him?
3. How would it smell in an ark with all those animals for that many days?
4. Did God keep Noah safe?
5. God promised a rainbow. Do you still see rainbows today?

Lesson
God was very sad about how people acted. He saved Noah and his family because their actions pleased Him. God has promised never to flood Earth again. The rainbow is God's sign to remind us of this promise. Although we make mistakes and turn away from God, He will not destroy us or Earth.

Use with *Sodom and Gomorrah* (page 18). Make two copies of Lot's wife. Cover one with white glitter to look like a pillar of salt.

Lot

Lot's Wife

Lot's Daughters

Angel

Angel

Use with *Sodom and Gomorrah* (page 18). Cut on the heavy black lines around three sides of the door and fold on the dotted line.

Cut patches for men's eyes from black construction paper.

Use with *Sodom and Gomorrah* (page 18). Make two copies, color, cut out, and attach to the shoebox as shown on page 18.

Use with *Sodom and Gomorrah* (page 18). Copy this page. Color the flames red, yellow, and orange. Cut them out and, at the end of the poem, attach them with removable adhesive to the cities.

22   *Bible Story Puppets and Poems*

Use with *Joseph and His Brothers* (page 26). Use removable adhesive to attach Joseph's coat and Jacob's tear. Attach the wheat to the shoebox as shown on page 26.

Joseph

Jacob's tear

Glue this Joseph inside pit.

Glue Jacob to a craft stick.

Use with *Joseph and His Brothers* (page 26). Glue all of Joseph's brothers to a glove as shown on page 26.

Use with *Joseph and His Brothers* (page 26).

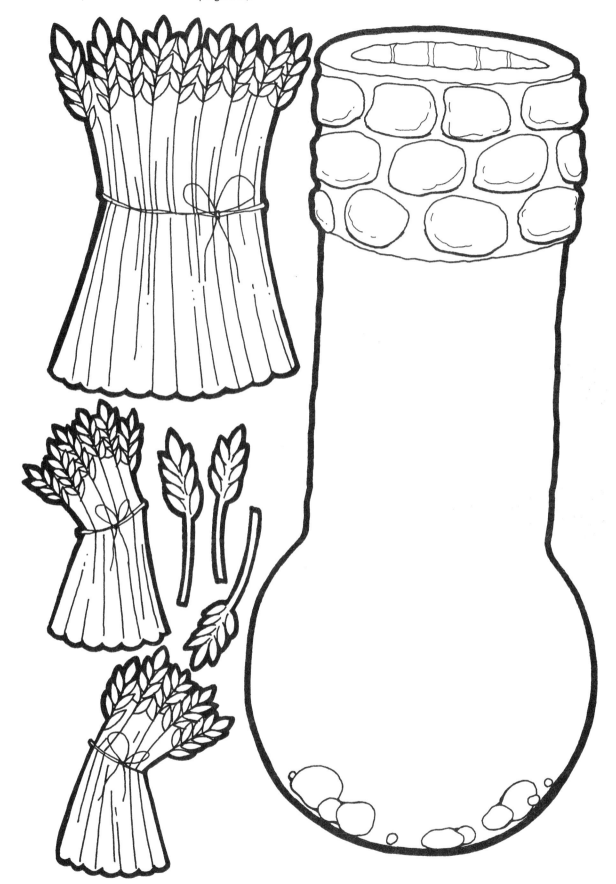

(Use the shoebox from Joseph and His Brothers (page 26) for the first three stanzas of the poem. Use the royal set (see bottom right) from Esther, Queen of Persia (pages 69 and 70) beginning in the fourth stanza.)

Do you remember Joseph
whose brothers threw him in a pit?
Well, he was away in Egypt
alive and keeping fit.

Joseph appears in pit.
Joseph leaves the pit.

Back home his family was starving;
they hardly had any food.
They would have eaten anything
baked, boiled, or stewed!

Joseph's family appears.

Now, Father Jacob heard that
in Egypt there was grain.
So he told his boys to go there
and see what they could gain.

Jacob talks to sons.

Benjamin leaves. Other sons go to Egypt.

They went to the governor of Egypt
to ask for help and bread.
They did not seem to know him.
They thought Joseph was dead.

Joseph appears.

The governor was actually Joseph,
their long lost kin.
He was so glad
to see his brothers again.

Joseph moves up and down.

He wanted to help them,
but first they had to pass a test.
He needed to see if they could change
and actually be honest.

Brothers take grain.
Silver cup appears in the bundle of grain.

They passed the test by bringing back
their young brother Ben
and by returning silver
that Joseph had planted on them.

Brothers go home.
Brothers return to Joseph with Benjamin.
They return silver cup to Joseph.

Pharaoh and Joseph were pleased
and welcomed them with zest.
Pharaoh cared for Joseph's family
and gave them Egypt's best!

Pharaoh and Joseph appear.

Members of Pharaoh's court appear.
Everyone stands together.

Questions
1. Was Joseph dead like his father thought?
2. Where was Joseph?
3. Who was hungry and needed food?
4. Did Joseph give his brothers the food they needed?
5. Did Joseph forgive his brothers?

Lesson
Joseph was still alive and was in charge of many things in Egypt. His brothers needed food and he could help them. He forgave them for what they had done. He still loved them and gave them food. God wants you to be like Joseph. It pleases God when we forgive and love our enemies.

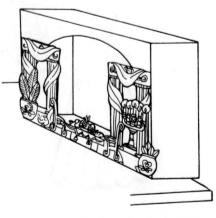

Use with *Joseph Remembers His Brothers* (page 30). Use removable adhesive to attach grain and silver cup to puppets. Make copies of grain for the last line of the poem. Glue the family pattern to a craft stick.

Pharaoh

Joseph

Jacob

In Egypt the king commanded
that all baby boys should die.
He demanded they be thrown in the river.
He wasn't a very nice guy.

A Levite woman had a son
and lived in faithful ways.
She cared for him in secret
for ninety precious days.

Moses' mother appears.
Mother holds Moses.

She places him behind her.

The baby thrived in secret.
He continued to grow.
His mother kept him hidden
so people wouldn't know.

She put him in a basket
and put the basket in the Nile.
His sister stood quietly
and watched him quite a while.

Basket is in the reeds.
Mother moves away.
Sister watches him.

Pharaoh's daughter and her maidens
took a little trip.
They walked down to the Nile
so the daughter could take a dip.

Pharaoh's daughter and maiden appear.

They walk behind the reeds.

Pharaoh's daughter saw the basket
and sent a maiden to find out
just who was in the basket
and what the crying was about.

Maiden walks to and looks in the basket.

The baby's sister asked the maiden
if she should get him a nurse.
Pharaoh's daughter said, "I'll pay"
and went to get her purse.

Moses' sister speaks to maiden.
Pharaoh's daughter gets her purse.

So the baby returned
to his very own mother.
She was, of course, the best nurse for him,
better than any other.

Moses returns to his mother.

As the baby boy grew older,
he was sent to Pharaoh's daughter.
She then named him Moses, which means
"I drew him out of water."

Moses' mother gives him to Pharaoh's daughter.

Questions
1. Who put Moses in a basket in the river?
2. Why did she put him there?
3. Did Moses drown in the river?
4. Who found him and took care of him?
5. Did Moses grow up?

Lesson
The king in Egypt wanted all baby boys killed. Moses' mother loved him very much and, like other mothers, did not want her son to die. She put her son in a basket in the Nile River so someone would find him and care for him. Moses' parents knew that he was no ordinary child. They were not afraid of the king's edict. God is pleased when we, like Moses' parents, have faith, not fear.

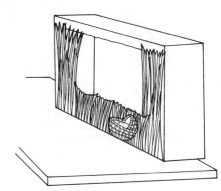

Use with *Moses in the Nile* (page 32). Attach Moses to the basket and the basket to the reeds with removable adhesive.

Pharaoh's daughter

Moses' Mother

Moses' Sister

Use with *Moses in the Nile* (page 32). Copy this page to create two sections of tall reeds and two sections of short reeds. Cut, color, and attach them to the shoebox as shown on page 32.

Maiden

Moses led a flock of sheep
into the desert one day.
He came to a place called Horeb,
and decided to stay.

Moses appears.
Sheep appear near the stage.

Moses arrives at the mountain.

Moses saw an angel
in the flame of a bush burning bright.
He could barely believe his eyes.
It was quite an amazing sight!

Angel appears in the burning bush.

The bush kept on burning,
but it did not burn away.
God wanted Moses' attention
because He had something to say.

God said, "Take off your sandals,
you're standing on holy ground.
I want to help my people
so they can become unbound."

Moses removes his sandals.

Israelites (page 40) appear.

"I'm choosing you to go to Pharaoh
and set my people free.
I don't like how he's treating them.
It's not okay with me."

Pharaoh (page 39) appears.

God told Moses to tell Pharaoh
that he was sent by the great I Am.
He said he would help him
if he got into a jam.

Moses listens to God.

With his brother and a staff,
Moses stood up to Pharaoh.
Pharaoh had a change of heart
and let God's people go!

Moses faces Pharaoh.

Israelites rejoice.

Questions
1. Where did Moses see an angel?
2. Have you ever seen an angel?
3. Does God talk to you? If so, how?
4. What did God want Moses to do?
5. Did he do it?

Lesson
God talked to Moses through an angel in a burning bush. God still speaks to people today. Instead of talking to you through a burning bush, He might talk to you through some quiet time, a song, a story, or a friend. When you hear God's voice, stop, be still, and listen. Trust that the Lord will help you to hear His voice.

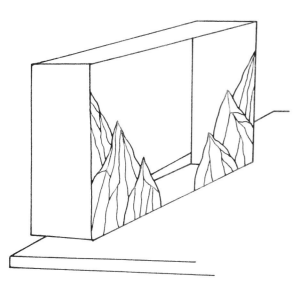

Use with *Moses and the Burning Bush* (page 35). Use removable adhesive to attach sandals to Moses and the sheep to the mountains.

Moses

Use with *Moses and the Burning Bush* (page 35). Copy, color, cut out, and attach mountains to the shoebox as shown on page 35.

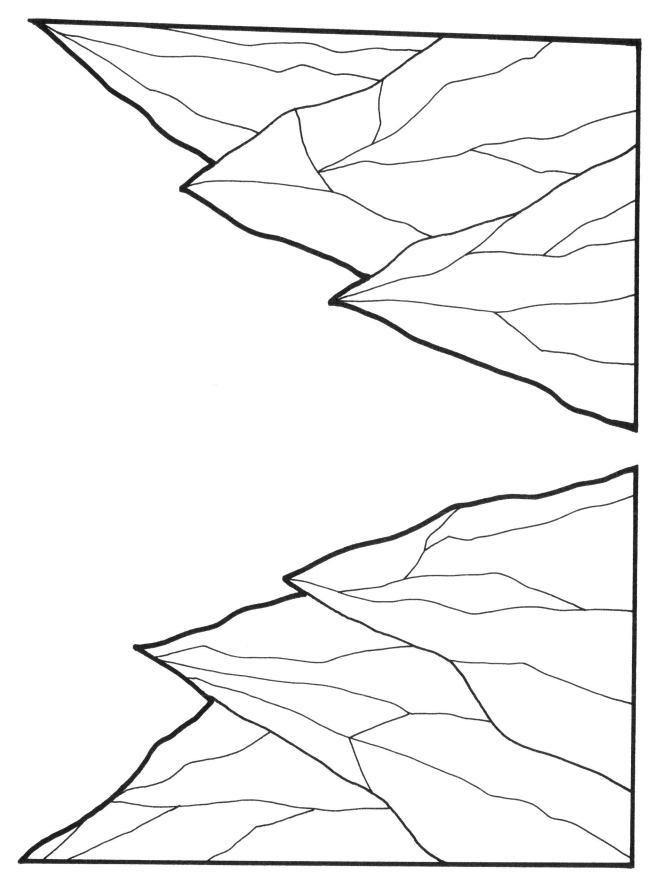

Moses Parts the Sea
Exodus 13–14

When Pharaoh finally gave in
and let the Israelites go,
God sent them through the desert.
The journey was very slow.

Pharaoh appears.
Moses and Israelites appear.
They move slowly through the desert.

The Lord was with them as a cloud
each and every day.
He went up ahead of them
to guide them on their way.

Cloud appears.

Cloud moves ahead of the Israelites.

The Lord was a pillar of fire.
He was with them every night.
He traveled with them in this way
to guide and give them light.

Pillar of fire appears.

Pillar of fire moves ahead of the Israelites.

Then, one night the Israelites
camped beside the sea.
Pharaoh came after them—
he and his whole army!

Israelites and Moses lay down and rest.

Pharaoh appears.
Egyptian army appears.

The Israelites started to worry
and they began to squirm.
Moses said, "The Lord will help us.
Just be patient and stand firm."

Israelites stand up and look towards the oncoming army.

Moses stands up.

Then, God said to Moses,
"Raise your staff; stretch your hand."
As Moses lifted it high,
the wet sea turned to dry land.

Moses raises his staff.

The Israelites then passed through
walking on dry ground.
Moses stretched his hand again,
and the Egyptian army drowned.

Israelites move through the sea.

Egyptians drown.

The Israelites saw the Lord's power
and decided that they must
follow His servant Moses
and give God their trust.

Moses stands apart.
Israelites look at Moses.

Questions
1. The Israelites were afraid when Pharaoh's army was following them. Would you be worried, too?
2. Can you picture the water moving out of the way so the Israelites could cross?
3. What did God tell Moses to do to make the waters move apart?
4. Was God protecting Moses and the Israelites?
5. What happened to Pharaoh's army?

Lesson
The Israelites had been through so much—slavery, hunger, and more. When Pharaoh's army appeared, the people thought that the journey from slavery to freedom was in vain. God knew that the journey was hard and had mercy on the Israelites. God wants us to be merciful like Him. When family members or friends are hurting, the Lord is pleased when we show mercy and compassion.

Use with *Moses Parts the Sea* (page 38). Attach Moses' staff to his hand with removable adhesive. Glue fire to a craft stick and move it ahead of Israelites as God travels with them at night.

Moses

Pharaoh

Bible Story Puppets and Poems

Use with *Moses Parts the Sea* (page 38). Glue Israelites, soldiers, and the cloud to craft sticks.

Use with *Moses Parts the Sea* (page 38). Copy, color blue, cut out, and attach to the shoebox as shown on page 38.

41

Jericho was tightly shut.
It was closed without a doubt.
No one could come in,
and no one could go out.

Doors remain closed.

God said, "March once 'round the city
six days in a row.
On day seven, march seven times
and let those trumpets blow!

Joshua appears.

Joshua gets a trumpet.

When the mighty trumpets blast,
be brave and do not doubt.
Get your group together
and have the people shout!"

Joshua remains standing.

People appear near Joshua.

So, for six days 'round the city,
Joshua's group made one trip, not two!
They marched and blew the horns
as God had said to do!

Joshua and people go around the city 6 times.

Trumpets sound.

They spared Rahab and her family.
They thought it would be wise,
since she had helped the Israelites
by hiding two of their spies.

On the seventh day, they circled
seven times around.
All at once they gave a shout
at the trumpets' sound.

They walk around the city 7 times.

Trumpets sound and people shout.

The wall began to crumble
at the people's yell.
The buildings toppled down
and the wall of Jericho fell.

Wall crumbles.

Blocks topple.

Questions
1. Have you ever seen a whole city fall down?
2. Did Joshua and his army need bombs to make the walls fall?
3. Who really made the walls fall?
4. Did Joshua and the people obey God?
5. Who was saved besides Joshua and the Israelites?

Lesson
Joshua and the Israelites trusted God even though they did not understand every part of God's plan. They had faith, did as God told them to do, and accomplished a mighty task. People have goals and are sometimes unsure of how to reach them. When you ask for help, God hears your cry and provides guidance in different ways—people, answers, and sometimes more questions. When people of faith journey together to follow Him, astonishing things happen.

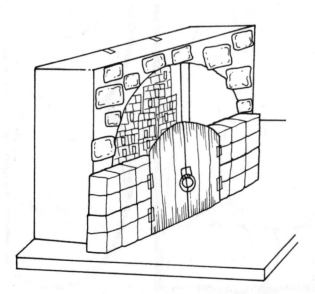

Use with *Joshua and the Fall of Jericho* (page 42). Use removable adhesive to attach the trumpet to Joshua and the stones to the shoebox as shown on page 42. Glue the Israelites to a craft stick.

Joshua

Use with *Joshua and the Fall of Jericho* (page 42). Copy, color, cut out, and glue Jericho to the inside of the lid as shown on page 42.

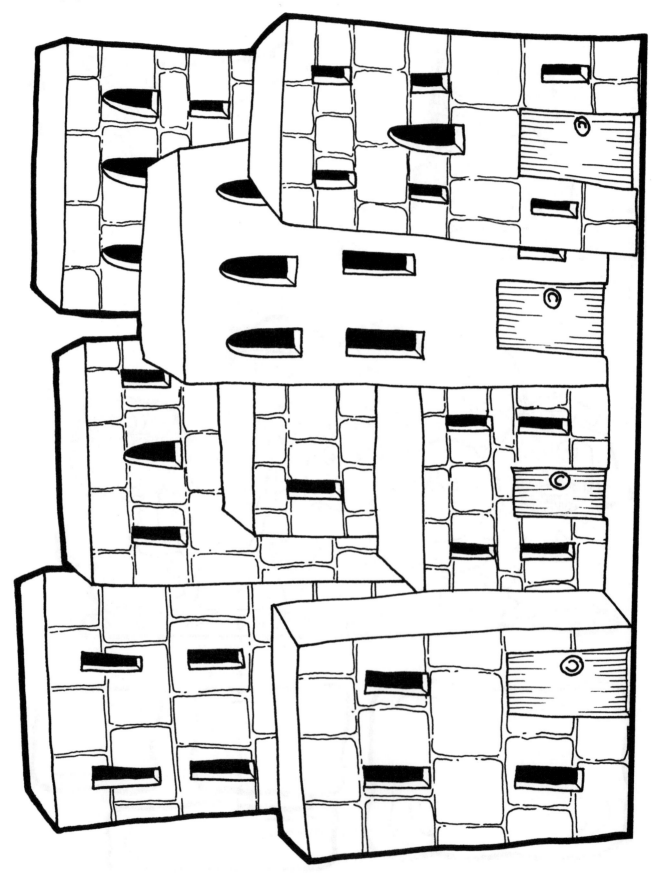

Bible Story Puppets and Poems

Use with *Joshua and the Fall of Jericho* (page 42). Copy the block pattern 24 times. Fold and tape the edges to make blocks. Stack the blocks in front of the shoebox as shown on page 42.

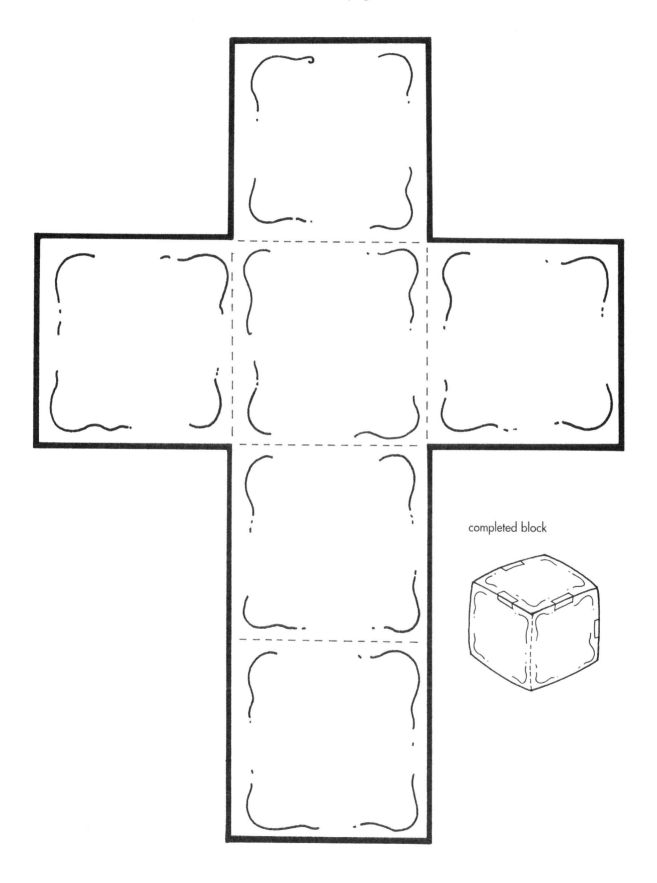

completed block

Use with *Joshua and the Fall of Jericho* (page 42). Attach the gate to the blocks in front of the shoebox as shown on page 42.

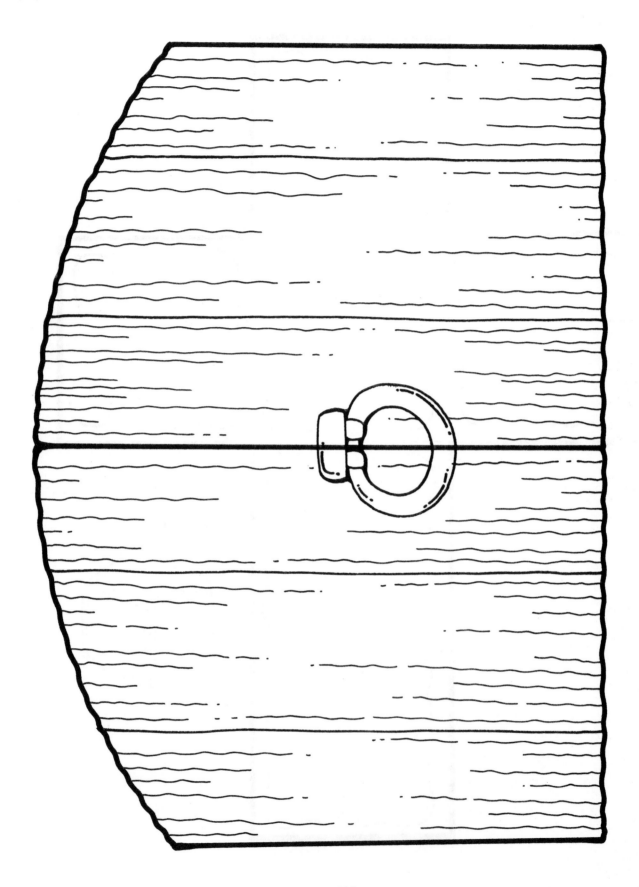

 Bible Story Puppets and Poems

Deborah was leading Israel.
She was a prophetess.
She heard the cries of citizens
and stated what was best.

Deborah appear.

Arguers appear.

Deborah summoned Barak
and told him the Lord said to go.
He'd deliver Jabin's army
and they would suffer woe!

Barak and ten thousand men
were to follow God's command.
God would deliver Sisera
into Barak's hand.

Barak appears.

Barak didn't want to go
to Kedesh on his own.
He wanted Deborah to go, too,
so he wouldn't be alone.

Barak paces.

Barak faces Deborah.

So Deborah went with him,
and the Lord was on their side.
They faced Jabin's army
and many soldiers died.

They walk away.

Army falls.

The other army's leader, Sisera,
quickly ran away.
Jael asked him to come in,
knowing he would stay.

Sisera appears.
Sisera runs away.
Jael appears.

Jael knew Sisera was cruel
so she killed him in his sleep.
Even though he was dead,
she thought no one would weep.

Jael and Sisera appear.

Sisera dies and is covered with a blanket.

Questions
1. What was Deborah's job?
2. What kind of leader was Sisera?
3. Who wanted Deborah to go with him to battle?
4. Who helped the Israelites win the battle against Jabin's army?

Lesson
Sisera, the commander of King Jabin's army, had oppressed the Israelites for many years. The Israelites cried to God for help. Deborah, the leader of Israel, sent for Barak to lead soldiers in battle. When Sisera found out about the plan, he gathered his army to fight. Sisera fled during the battle to the tent of Jael, the wife of Heber the Kenite. Sisera was so exhausted that he fell asleep and then Jael killed him. This story reveals how God delivered the Israelites from their enemies in an unusual way.

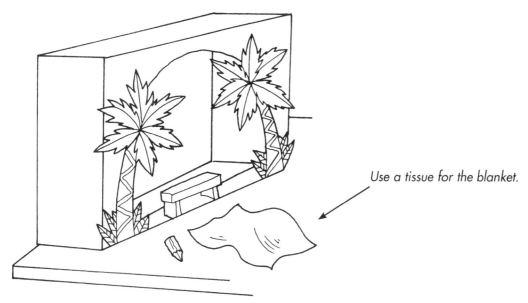

Use a tissue for the blanket.

Use with *Deborah and Barak* (page 47). Make two copies of the palm tree. Place the trees and the bench on the shoebox as shown on page 47. Copy the army (page 51) to use with this poem.

Deborah

Use with *Deborah and Barak* (page 47).

Jael

Arguer 1

Arguer 2

Barak

Sisera

Bible Story Puppets and Poems

There was an Israelite army
led by a man named Gideon.
God wanted the army to fight
and destroy the camp of Midian.

Israelite army appears.
Gideon stands in front.

The Lord told Gideon
he had too many men to fight.
With fewer soldiers in battle,
they must trust God's might.

Gideon listens to God.

So Gideon told the soldiers,
"If you're afraid, you may go back."
Twenty-two thousand went home.
Ten thousand stayed to attack.

Army moves away.
Army returns.

But the Lord said, "That's still too many
to win this fight, I think.
Keep the men who lap the water
when they get a drink."

Army moves away.

Three hundred Israelites were left.
Three hundred was all there were,
but God told Gideon they could win.
Of that fact He was sure!

Army returns.

Gideon gave each man a trumpet
and a jar with a torch inside.
They blew horns and broke jars
with Gideon as their guide.

Men get trumpets.
Men get jars.
Trumpets sound and the jars break.

Grasping their torches and trumpets,
they began to shout,
"For the Lord and for Gideon!"
The Midianites' time had run out!

Army rejoices.

Army faces Gideon.

Questions
1. Who was the leader of the Israelite army?
2. Did the army have lots of men?
3. Did the army stay the same size?
4. Why didn't Gideon need all of his men?
5. How could Gideon win the battle with trumpets and jars?

Lesson
Gideon began a battle with a huge army. God wanted the power to be attributed to Him, not to the size of the army, so God asked Gideon to let some men return home. He cut the size of his army two times. He could win if God was on his side. You don't have to have the largest army in the world to win if you have God. You don't have to be the biggest or fastest. There's nothing you can do to make God love you any more than He already does.

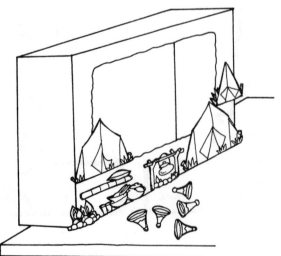

Use with *Gideon and His Army* (page 50). Glue Gideon's army to a craft stick. Scatter the jars below and the trumpets on the next page on the table close to the shoebox.

Gideon

Use with *Gideon and His Army* (page 50). Attach the props on this page, except for the trumpets, to the shoebox with removable adhesive as shown on page 50.

(Perform poem away from temple set.)

Samson was born strong.
His strength was in his hair.
He was stronger than everyone.
It didn't quite seem fair.

Samson appears.
His hair gets longer.

He braced himself against the pillars
and pushed with one great thrust.
The temple fell to the ground
and crushed everything like dust.

Samson met a woman.
Delilah was her name.
He fell in love with her
and would never be the same.

Delilah appears.

They stand together.

*Temple falls over. Optional: Stack blocks (page **45**) and topple them over.*

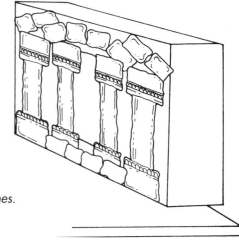

The Philistines told Delilah
to find out why Samson was strong.
She devised a wicked plan;
it didn't take her very long.

Philistines appear.

First he said to tie him—
tie him up with seven strings.
Samson broke them all
as if there were no such things.

Samson is tied with string.

Samson breaks strings.

Three times Delilah asked him
and three times Samson lied.
Delilah tried to get an answer.
She tried and tried and tried.

Delilah goes to Samson three times.

Delilah kept on asking him
each and every day.
She asked until Samson gave up
and gave his secret away.

Delilah nags Samson.

So Delilah put his head in her lap
and lulled him fast to sleep.
A man came in and shaved his hair.
Samson didn't hear a peep!

Samson tells his secret.

Samson falls asleep.

Hair falls away.

Questions
1. What made Samson strong?
2. Was Delilah a nice woman?
3. Should Samson have told her his secret?
4. What did the Philistines do to Samson?
5. Who made Samson strong again?

The Philistines came and took him
and punched him in the eyes.
They bound him with bronze chains.
He was very surprised.

Philistines carry Samson off.
They add shackles.
They leave. Samson falls.

Samson didn't stay captive long.
His hair began to grow.
He'd show those Philistines
that he was still their foe.

Samson stands up.
His hair grows back.

Lesson
Samson's gift from God was his strength. Samson was tricked by Delilah to tell her about his gift and the Philistines thought they could take his strength away. Samson did the right thing by praying to God. God gave him his strength back and then Samson destroyed the Philistines. Remember to pray to God, like Samson did, and trust God to help you!

They took him to their temple
where he prayed, "Remember me."
They put him beneath the pillars
where thousands of people could see.

Everyone goes to the temple.

*Bible Story Puppets and **Poems***

Use with *Samson's Strength* (page 53). Attach hair and shackles to Samson and scissors to Delilah with removable adhesive. Glue Philistines to the fingers of a cotton glove as shown below.

Samson

Delilah

Use with *Samson's Strength* (page 53). Make two copies of this page. For added drama, stack the blocks (page 45) next to the shoebox.

Naomi's husband died,
but she had two sons
who had married Moabite women—
Ruth and Orpah were the ones.

Naomi appears.

Ruth appears and then Orpah appears.

They lived in Moab nearly 10 years
before both of Naomi's sons died.
She tried to get them to go home,
but they wanted to stay by her side.

Naomi faces Ruth and Orpah.

Finally Naomi convinced Orpah,
and she went on her way.
Ruth said, "Where you go, I will go
and where you stay, I will stay."

Orpah turns and moves away.
Ruth faces Naomi.

So Ruth and Naomi
to Bethlehem did go.
They went to harvest in the fields
where wheat and barley grow.

Ruth and Naomi go in the fields.

Grain is added.

Ruth followed the harvesters
and walked along behind.
This is where she met Boaz,
a man so sweet and kind.

Naomi disappears. Ruth stays in fields.
Ruth moves back and forth across the fields.
Boaz appears.

Boaz wanted to help them both,
so for them he did provide.
He bought their land and wanted Ruth
to be his lovely bride.

Naomi returns.

Boaz and Ruth stand.

Boaz was so happy that
he took young Ruth to wed,
and soon Ruth had a baby boy,
whom they named Obed.

Boaz kisses Ruth.
Ruth holds Obed.
All stand together.

Questions

1. What bad things happened to Naomi?
2. Did Orpah go back home? Did Ruth?
3. What did Ruth do?
4. Who helped Ruth and Naomi?
5. Was Ruth good to Naomi?

Lesson

Naomi was all alone. Her husband and both sons had died. Ruth was still a young woman. Although Ruth could have returned home, she chose to stay with Naomi. Together, they started a new life. When friends are lonely and times are tough, God hopes that we will be there for them. Sometimes the best thing we can do is be present for one another in times of need. God is pleased when we, like Naomi, give up something in order to help others.

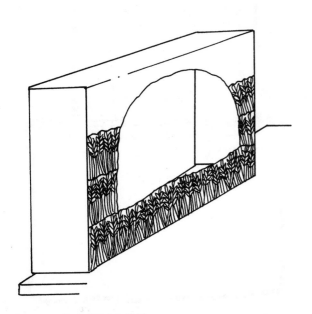

Use with *Naomi and Ruth* (page 56). Use removable adhesive to attach baby Obed to Ruth's arm.

Use with *Naomi and Ruth* (page 56).

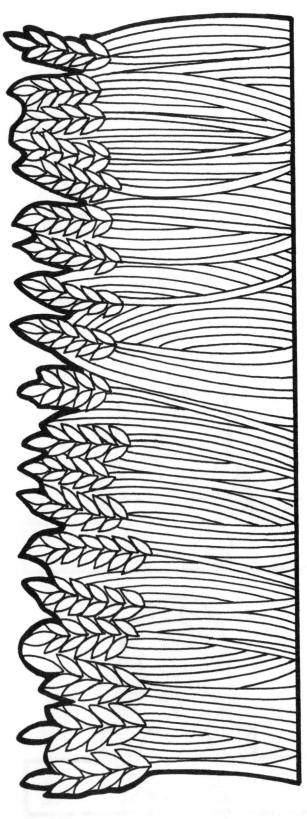

David Chosen as King
I Samuel 16

David was a shepherd boy.
He watched over the sheep.
He watched them day and night
and sometimes didn't sleep.

David watches sheep.

Sun and moon appear.

One day Samuel sent
for all of Jesse's sons but one.
He was the small boy David,
Jesse's youngest son.

Other sons appear.

Samuel said, "No,
the Lord has not chosen these.
Bring the other son
for me to look at, please."

Samuel shakes head "no."
Samuel points towards David.

Next to his group of brothers,
David was small,
yet in the eyes of God,
he was mighty and tall!

David appears next to his brothers.

David gets taller.

God told Samuel to
please be smart.
"Don't just look at the outside.
Look at the boy's heart!"

Samuel sees David's heart.

Samuel then chose David
to be the very next king.
This choice was the best;
it had the Lord's blessing.

David gets the crown.

David bows.

Questions
1. What was David doing at the beginning of the poem?
2. Which of Jesse's sons did Samuel choose to be the next king?
3. Was David big and strong?
4. What did God want Samuel to look at?
5. Are people different from what you see on the outside of them?

Lesson
God chose David to be the next king. Even though David was young and small, God looked at his heart. God knew that David was good and had special gifts. People come in all shapes and sizes, but we are all God's children. Each one of us is a special child of God. God is pleased when we consider who people are instead of what they look like.

Use with *David Chosen as King* (page 59). Attach David's brothers to a craft stick as shown below. Use removable adhesive to attach the crown and the heart to David.

David

Samuel

eye pattern

ear pattern

Make sheep from cotton balls. Using the ear pattern, trace and cut the ears from black construction paper. Use the eye pattern provided or glue on wiggly eyes. Glue sheep to the fingertips of a cotton glove.

Use with *David Chosen as King* (page 59).

The Philistines had a warrior
who really wanted to fight.
He was nine feet tall, mean,
and really quite a fright.

Goliath appears.

Goliath stood
and began to shout,
"Hey you Israelites,
send a warrior out!"

Goliath shouts.

For 40 days
Goliath took his stand,
until David, visiting his brothers,
entered the land.

David appears.

David said,
"I will take your dare.
As a shepherd,
I killed both a lion and a bear."

David speaks.

Then, David put on armor
and a helmet for his head,
but then he took them off.
He wasn't used to them, he said.

David puts on armor and helmet.
David takes off armor and helmet.

David chose five smooth stones,
a pouch, his staff, and sling.
With these weapons in hand,
he took on the Philistine.

He gets pouch, staff, and sling.

David bows.

The giant moved closer
to make a strong attack,
but bold and daring David
did not shrink back.

Goliath moves closer.

David faces Goliath.

David slung a stone
that hit the giant in the head.
The Philistines ran away.
Their hero was dead.

Stone hits Goliath's head.
Crowd leaves.
Goliath dies.

Questions
1. What was the name of the Philistine giant?
2. Was he strong and tough?
3. Who had better weapons to fight with—David or Goliath?
4. With what did David kill Goliath?
5. How do you think David beat Goliath?

Lesson
David was brave. He killed both a lion and a bear to protect his sheep. Even though the giant had armor and weapons, David killed him with just one small stone. David had faith that God would be with him and protect him. God is pleased when you show that you trust Him. No matter where you are or what is happening to you, remember that God will protect you and be with you always.

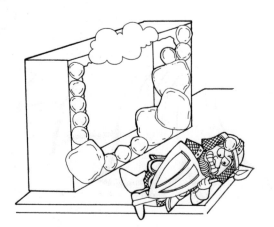

Use with *David and Goliath* (page 62). Use removable adhesive to attach David's armor and weapons. Glue the Philistines to a craft stick.

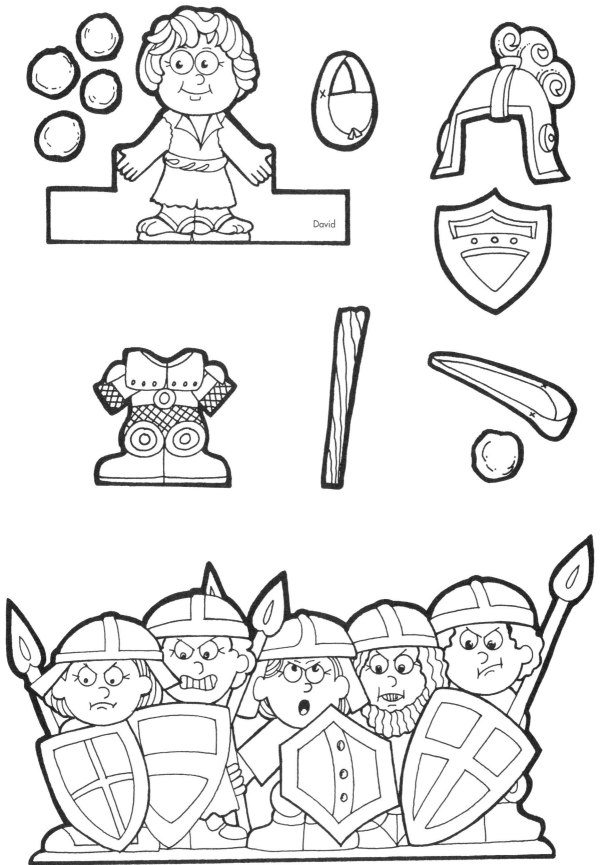

David

Use with *David and Goliath* (page 62). Use removable adhesive to attach the cloud and the rocks to the shoebox as shown on page 62.

Use shoebox from Esther, Queen of Persia (pages 69 and 70).

Israel pleaded for God
to send them a mighty king.
Saul received the power
to rule over everything.

Saul gets crowned.

Some of the Lord's commands
Saul did not obey,
so an evil spirit
visited him each day.

Tablets appear.

Evil spirit appears.
Saul shakes with fear.

David was sent to play the harp.
Each day he played a tune.
Each time Saul heard it,
he'd feel better soon.

David gets his harp.

Evil spirit leaves Saul.

Then, David slew Goliath,
the giant fierce and tall.
The people called David
the greatest warrior of them all.

Goliath (page 64) appears.
David knocks him over.

Now, Saul did not like this.
It didn't make him glad.
He was jealous of David.
It nearly drove him mad.

Saul was quite unhappy.
He wanted David dead.
He even took a spear
and hurled it toward David's head.

Evil spirit returns to Saul.

Evil spirit leaves.

David has a spear above his head.

Saul gave one of his daughters
to David for a wife,
but this didn't change a thing.
Saul still wanted David's life!

Saul had a son named Jonathan
who became David's lifelong friend.
He warned David to hide from Saul
or else his life would end.

Saul chases David.

Jonathan appears.

Jonathan faces David.

David could have killed Saul,
but twice his life he spared.
Saul was finally thankful and
showed David that he cared.

David stands near Saul.

Saul bows to David.

Questions
1. Who helped Saul feel better?
2. What did David do to make him feel better?
3. Why did Saul stop liking David?
4. David could have killed Saul two times. Do you think he should have?
5. Did Saul like David again?

Lesson
David's job was to play music to help Saul feel better. David then killed Goliath and won many wars. All the people bragged about David. This made Saul so jealous and angry that he wanted to kill David. David still honored Saul because he was the king. Even though Saul was after his life, David refused to kill him. Finally, Saul forgave him. God invites us to be like David and respect our leaders.

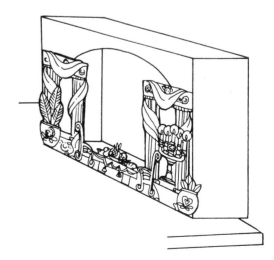

Use with *David and Saul* (page 65). Use the stage from *Esther, Queen of Persia* (pages 69 and 70) for this poem. Attach the evil spirit to a craft stick. Use removable adhesive to attach the tablets to the shoebox, the crown to Saul's head, and the harp to David.

Saul

Jonathan

David

Esther, Queen of Persia
Esther 2-8

King Xerxes was a rich king
who wanted a new queen.
He looked at all the young girls
to pick a beautiful teen.

King Xerxes appears.

Young girls appear.

The king saw Esther, Mordecai's cousin,
and quickly shared his favor,
so a year of beauty treatments
and special food she would savor.

Esther and Mordecai appear.
Mordecai leaves.
Esther gets a facial.
Her facial is complete and she wears the crown.

Mordecai, a Jew like Esther,
heard guards' plan to kill the king.
Mordecai told Esther,
who told Xerxes everything.

King Xerxes rewarded Mordecai
for sharing the guards' plot.
He gave Mordecai a royal robe
and a horse with a crest to trot.

The king said, "Honor Haman,"
but Mordecai did not bow his head.
He followed Jewish law
and bowed to God instead.

King stands next to Haman.
Mordecai appears.
Mordecai shakes his head "no."

Esther dined with Haman and the king
and shared Haman's evil plan.
King Xerxes granted her request
and better life for Jews began.

Queen Esther appears.
Haman and King sit near Esther.

King Xerxes spared her people
and wrote an edict for the Jews.
Thanks to Queen Esther,
they finally heard good news.

Esther stands in front.

Esther bows.

Questions
1. Who did Esther marry?
2. How was Mordecai related to Esther?
3. Who did Haman want to kill?
4. Who asked the king to save the Jews?

Lesson
King Xerxes chose Esther for his wife. Mordecai, Esther's cousin, shared that two of the king's guards were planning to kill him. Haman tried to get the king to order the Jews' destruction. The king did not know that Mordecai and Esther were Jews. The king then sent a message to destroy all Jews on a given day. The king honored Mordecai for telling him about the conspiracy. Then, Esther invited the king and Haman to a banquet. There, she shared Haman's plan and convinced Xerxes to spare her people. God wants us to be like Esther. He is pleased when we stand up for others.

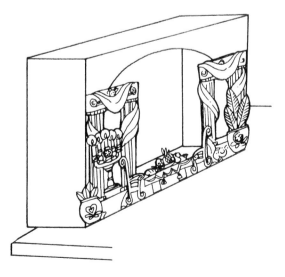

Bible Story Puppets and Poems

Use with *Esther, Queen of Persia* (page 67). Use removable adhesive to attach the new robe to Mordecai and the beauty mask and the crown to Esther.

Esther

Mordecai

Haman

King Xerxes

young girls

Use with *Esther, Queen of Persia* (page 67). Copy, color, cut out, and attach these items to the shoebox as shown on page 67.

Use with *Esther, Queen of the Jews* (page 67). Make two copies of this page.

Nebuchadnezzar's a bad guy
so, so, so,
"We won't worship gold.
No, no, no!"
said Shadrach, Meshach, and Abednego.

Nebuchadnezzar appears.

Shadrach, Meshach, and Abednego appear.

"There's only one God
we know, know, know."
claimed Shadrach, Meshach, and Abednego.

Shadrach, Meshach, and Abednego nod as if saying "yes."

The king then asked,
"Is that so, so, so,
Shadrach, Meshach, and Abednego?"

Nebuchadnezzar speaks.

"You're making me angry,
so into the fiery furnace you go,
Shadrach, Meshach, and Abednego!"

In that fiery furnace were four,
oh, oh, oh,
one plus Shadrach, Meshach, and Abednego.

Shadrach, Meshach, and Abednego move through the flames into the box.

God's love will always
flow, flow, flow;
He'll keep you safe
as you go, go, go
like Shadrach, Meshach, and Abednego.

Shadrach, Meshach, and Abednego leave the furnace.

Questions
1. Nebuchadnezzar tried to get Shadrach, Meshach, and Abednego to do the wrong thing. What did he want them to do?
2. Did they do it? Why not?
3. What was their punishment?
4. Were they harmed by the fire?
5. Who protected Shadrach, Meshach, and Abednego in the furnace?

Lesson
Shadrach, Meshach, and Abednego worshiped God even though it meant they must go to the furnace. Although the king wanted them to worship him, they refused. God is pleased when we, like Shadrach, Meshach, and Abednego, put Him first in our lives. He is with us during trials and tribulations. God's love will help us through the tough times as we follow Him.

Use with *Shadrach, Meshach, and Abednego* (page 71). Copy stones and flames to decorate stage as shown on page 71. Glue Shadrach, Meshach, and Abednego to a glove. Glue the flames to the extra fingers of the first glove and to all fingers of another glove as shown on page 73. Copy the smoke pattern below twice.

Punch hole with a toothpick and run thread through the smoke pattern to hang from the top of the shoebox.

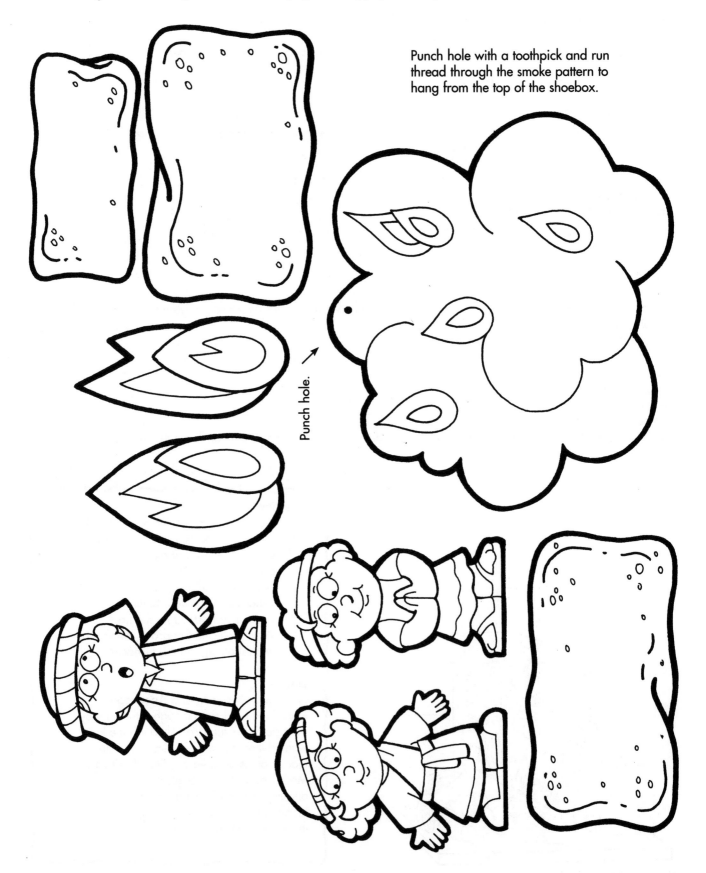

Punch hole.

Use with *Shadrach, Meshach, and Abednego* (page 71). Glue one copy of the smoke pattern (page 72) to a craft stick as shown below.

King Nebuchadnezzar

The king gave Daniel an important job
and he did it oh so well.
The other workers began to complain.
Some even began to yell.

Daniel appears.

King's men appear.

They wanted to make Daniel look bad,
but he was angelic and good.
Try as they might with all their schemes,
they never, ever could.

They told the king to write a law
so that all would pray to him.
Praying to another man or God
would make your future grim.

But Daniel prayed only to God
each and every day.
That's the way it had always been,
and how it would stay!

King leaves. Daniel prays.

Daniel got down on his knees
and prayed a prayer or two.
When the king's men caught him,
they said, "In the lions' den with you!"

Daniel is on his knees by his bed.

Bring king's men to take Daniel away.
They walk towards the lions' den.

They put Daniel in the den
and sealed it with a stone.
There with lions around him,
Daniel sat all alone.

They put Daniel in the den.
They seal the den.

Meanwhile the king could not sleep
and he certainly could not eat.
By morning's light he was afraid
that Daniel was lions' meat!

King appears restless.

Questions
1. Was Daniel a good worker for the king?
2. Did the other workers like him?
3. What law did they have the king make?
4. Did Daniel obey the new law?
5. What happened when Daniel kept praying to God?

Daniel prayed that God
would keep him from harm the lions posed.
God did so much more than that!
He kept the lions' mouths closed!

Daniel prays in the den.

Lesson
Daniel was a good worker and loyal to the king, but he thought it was more important to be loyal to God. He would not pray to the king, so the king sent him to the lions' den as a punishment. He prayed to God. God shut the lions' mouths to protect him. The king saw God's power and began to worship Him. Tell others how powerful God is, so that they will worship Him, too.

The king saw God save Daniel
and he was so impressed
that he told all people to worship God,
for He's the very best!

King points to Daniel.

Daniel prays.

Use with *Daniel in the Lions' Den* (page 74). Use removable adhesive to attach the stone to the lions' den and praying Daniel beside his bed. Glue the king's five men to the fingers of a glove.

Daniel

King Darius

    Bible Story Puppets and Poems

Use with *Daniel in the Lions' Den* (page 74). Copy, color, cut out, and glue Daniel's room to cardboard or the front of the shoebox.

Cut out.

Use with *Daniel in the Lions' Den* (page 74). Copy, color, cut out, and glue the lions' den to cardboard or the front of a shoebox. Apply removable adhesive to attach the stone door (page 75) to the den as shown below.

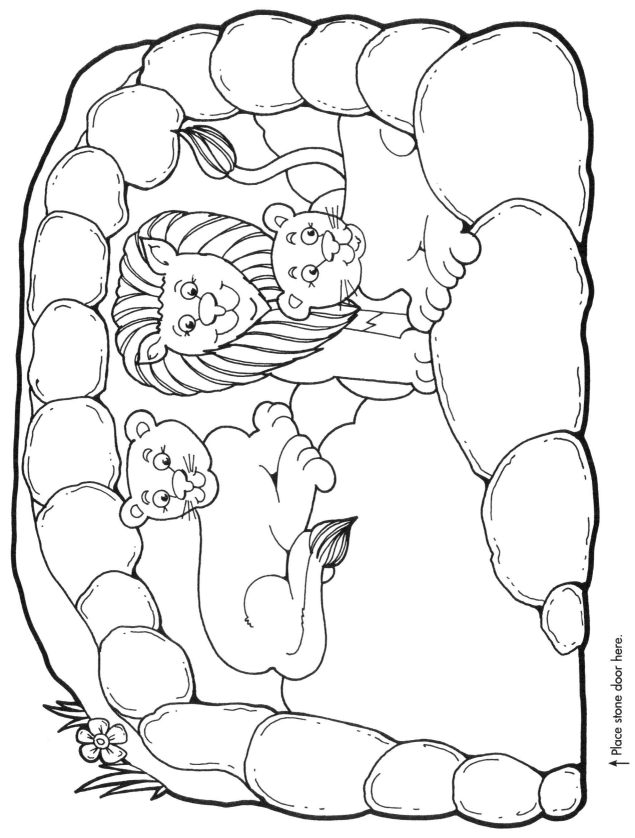

↑ Place stone door here.

God told Jonah
to spread the word,
but Jonah pretended
he hadn't heard.

After God spoke,
Jonah got on a boat
on its way to Tarshish,
a place very remote.

God never let Jonah
out of his sight.
He sent a storm.
It was an awful fright.

Jonah's shipmates
gave him a heave ho;
"Into the foaming ocean
you go!"

Oh, if Jonah could only
make one wish!
God beat him to it
and sent a big fish.

The fish ate Jonah
and there he lay.
In the fish's belly,
he began to pray!

Then, God saved Jonah
without a doubt.
The fish swam to shore
and spit him out!

Jonah appears above the stage.

Jonah disappears.

Jonah jumps off the ship.

Waves, boat, and people rock back and forth.

Jonah falls between the waves.

The fish appears.

The fish swallows Jonah.

Jonah leans forward.

Fish spits Jonah onto the shore.

Questions
1. Who told Jonah to spread the word?
2. Did Jonah listen?
3. What happened to Jonah?
4. Could he have died when he was eaten by the fish?
5. Why didn't Jonah die?

Lesson
God wanted Jonah to preach in a place called Nineveh, but Jonah refused. He traveled in the opposite direction to flee from God. God sent a great wind and after Jonah was thrown overboard, provided a great fish to rescue him. After Jonah prayed to God, the fish spat him out onto dry land. The great fish was not a punishment but a saving grace from God. God is pleased when we obey Him the first time, so that we can be in the right place at the right time to serve Him.

Use with *Jonah and the Big Fish* (page 78). Make two copies of this page. Attach one Jonah to a craft stick. Attach the other one with the four fish to the fingertips of a cotton glove. Use a wave and the other fish to decorate the shoebox. Glue the other wave and the boat to craft sticks as shown on page 78.

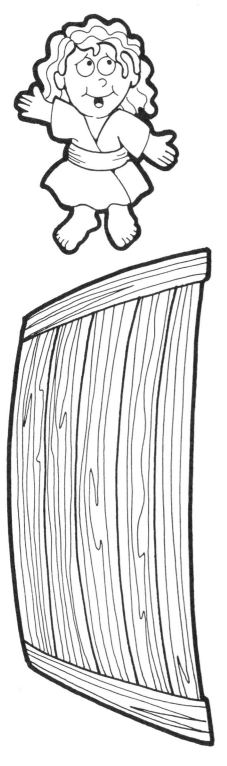

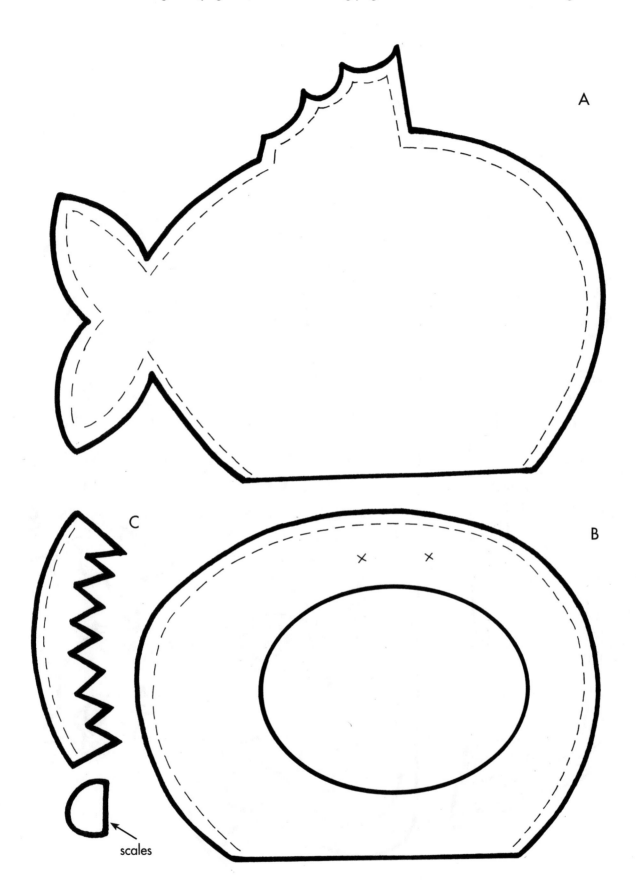

A

C

B

scales

Use with *Jonah and the Big Fish* (page 78).

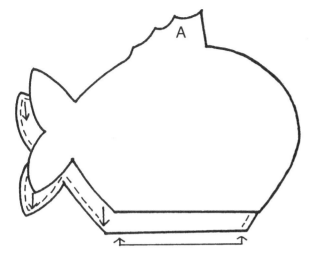

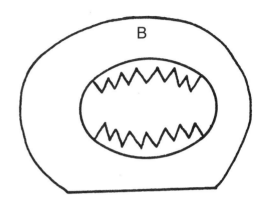

1. Cut two of piece A and glue together along dashed lines indicated on pattern.

2. Cut one B. Glue two of piece C (teeth) to underside as shown.

3. Glue B to top of A by gluing together along dashed lines.

4. Glue on wiggly eyes. Add fin and tail details with felt marker. Glue scales to fish and add sequins to scales.

Insert hand into back pocket of puppet. Insert finger with Jonah puppet into front pocket as needed.

(Start poem with puppets away from stage.)

Caesar asked for a census
to count how many people there were.
Every citizen had to go
to town and register.

Census paper appears.

Joseph went to register
and took Mary, his betrothed wife.
She was ready to have her child,
a baby who would bring new life!

Joseph appears.
Mary appears.

They looked for a cozy place.
The birth would soon begin,
but they had to stay in a stable.
There was no room at the inn!

They move towards the stable.

They enter the stable.

Shepherds in a field nearby
watched their flocks by night.
A child was born not far from them
to bring the world new light.

Shepherds watch flocks.

Jesus appears in the manger.
Manger appears in the stable.

To the shepherds in the field
an angel did appear.
The angel told the shepherds,
"Your Savior, Christ, is here!"

Angel appears.
Angel faces shepherds.
Angel speaks.

The shepherds didn't linger.
They hurried off to see.
They soon found Joseph and Mary
and the tiny, holy baby.

Shepherds walk to the stable.

Shepherds look at the three.

The shepherds went back home.
They were awestruck and dazed.
All the people who heard the Word
were especially amazed!

Shepherds leave.
Shepherds look to the heavens and bow.

Today, this day called Christmas
is celebrated on Earth,
but it became a holiday
because of Jesus' birth.

Flashlight shines on Jesus in the manger.

Questions
1. Where did Joseph and Mary have to spend the night?
2. Where were the shepherds?
3. Who told the shepherds that Jesus was born?
4. How does your family celebrate Christmas?

Lesson
On the night Jesus was born, an angel came to tell the shepherds about this very special baby. Jesus' birth wasn't special because he was born in a stable. It was special because he is the Savior of the world. It was special because God chose to take human form to dwell with us by sending Jesus. He came to Earth to teach a new way of life and to die for the sins of all people for all time. He is your Savior, too! Rejoice!

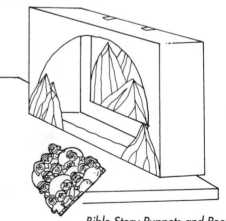

John the Baptist
Mark 1

(Use two shoeboxes for this poem. Place the desert scene on the left and the River Jordan scene on the right as shown below.)

John ate locusts and wild honey
and wore clothes of camel's hair.
He preached out in the desert.
People turned from their sins out there.

John the Baptist eats.

John preaches.

John was to prepare the way for Jesus
and to preach and to baptize.
So when Jesus came from Galilee,
it was really no surprise!

Jesus appears.

Should John baptize Jesus?
He thought maybe he was too rough,
but Jesus then assured him
that he was good enough.

John questions.
Question mark appears.
Question mark disappears.
Jesus and John go to the river.

When Jesus came out of the water,
God's spirit descended like a dove.
Then, God said, "This is my son,
the One whom I love."

Jesus comes out of the water.
Dove appears above Jesus.

Jesus' heart is visible.

Questions
1. What did John the Baptist eat?
2. What did he wear?
3. What was John doing in the desert?
4. What did John do for Jesus?
5. Was God happy about what John and Jesus had done?

Lesson
John the Baptist lived differently than many people during his time. People came to hear him preach in the desert and be baptized in the River Jordan. Jesus also came to be baptized by John. Baptism is a way of showing that you love God and you desire to follow Jesus. In baptism, we are marked as Christ's own forever. When you are baptized, you are blessed with the gift of water and the Holy Spirit. In essence, you are declaring your love for God and God is sharing His love for you. God is pleased when you are baptized and eager to follow the example of His son, Jesus.

Use with *John the Baptist* (page 89). Use removable adhesive to attach clothes, sandals, and the question mark to John the Baptist. Use removable adhesive to attach the heart and the dove to Jesus. Attach the rocks and the bush to the shoebox for the desert scene as shown on page 89.

John the Baptist

Jesus

Use with *John the Baptist* (page 89). Use the bare tree trunk for the desert scene. Attach the leafy treetops to the trunk (see below) for the River Jordan scene. Attach the waves, tree, and flowers for the River Jordan scene as shown on page 89.

Jesus gave a sermon.
It was called the Sermon on the Mount.
There were more people listening to it
than you could ever count!

Jesus appears.

Jesus stands in front of the crowd.
The crowd (page 103) listens to him.

He taught many good things
and all things that are right.
He told those who follow him
to be Earth's salt and light.

Jesus disappears.
Salt shaker and the light bulb appear.

Salt is used as seasoning
to flavor and preserve.
Jesus said to love our enemies,
give to others, and serve.

Salt shaker turns upside down and shakes.

Salt shaker disappears.

Always let your light shine
and keep it burning bright.
Let it burn so brightly that
it lights up half the night!

Light bulb moves up and down.

A city cannot be hidden
nor a lamp concealed under a bowl.
Put your light on a lamp stand
so its beam will forever glow!

Light bulb is covered by an audience member's hand.
Hand moves away from the light bulb.

Let men see your light shine
and also your good deeds.
Then, praise our Father in heaven
who meets all of our needs.

Flashlight shines.

Jesus reappears.

Questions
1. What's a sermon?
2. Why do people put salt on food?
3. How can people be "salt"?
4. Would you rather be alone in the light or in the dark?
5. How can you be a "light" to the world?

Lesson
Jesus wants those who believe in him to be like salt and light for the world. Salt is a seasoning that adds flavor to food and also preserves it. Jesus desires us to add flavor, or joy and wonder, to the lives of others. We are called to live a life of discipleship, to say prayers and live in right relationships with others. Light helps us see things more clearly and gives warmth. Jesus wants us to be light by sharing our unique gifts. God delights in you when you share your light, your gifts, and His goodness with others.

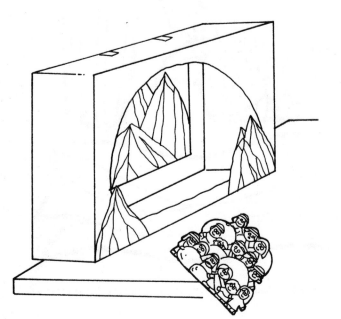

Use with *Salt and Light* (page 92). Use removable adhesive to attach the crowd (page 103) to one of the mountains. Make three copies of the mountains and attach them to the shoebox as shown on page 92.

Jesus

Light

Salt

Jesus and the Lame Man
Mark 2

Jesus came to Capernaum
to heal and to teach.
He spent his time with people,
hoping their hearts he'd reach.

Jesus appears.

People circle around him.

One day as Jesus was teaching
and healing those who were sick,
some men wanted to see him,
but the crowds were way too thick.

Jesus moves back and forth in front of crowd.
Jesus touches people.

Four men brought a man
who could not walk,
but they couldn't get close to Jesus,
not even to talk.

Men with friend on a mat appear.

They try to get near Jesus.
Others crowd around Jesus.

They couldn't get in to see Jesus
to have him heal their friend.
They took him through the roof
so that their long wait could end.

Men with friend go to the roof.
Men bring friend through the roof.

Jesus saw their faith
and forgave the paralytic's sin.
The Scribes didn't like it;
Only God could forgive the sins of men!

Jesus talks to them.

Scribes appear.

Jesus knew their thoughts.
"Why such thoughts would you let in?
Which is easier for me to do,
Heal the sick or forgive your sin?"

Jesus faces the Scribes.
He speaks to them.

Jesus said to the lame man,
"Now let's have no more talk.
I tell you, get up, take up your mat.
Take up your mat and walk."

Jesus faces the lame man.

The lame man promptly got up and
Jesus he did obey.
He walked where all could see him
on that very day.

The man walks.

He continues walking.

Everyone who was watching
couldn't believe their eyes.
They praised and worshiped God—
That's no surprise!

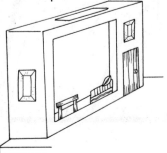

Questions
1. What does the word *lame* mean?
2. Who brought the lame man to Jesus?
3. How did they get their friend into the building?
4. Why did they go in that way?
5. Is a lame man becoming able to walk a good reason to praise God?

Lesson
The lame man's friends wanted to have him healed. They were willing to do whatever it took to get their friend to Jesus—even if it meant crawling in through the roof! Jesus knew they had great faith. He forgave their friend's sin and healed him, too. When we come to Jesus with our hurts and our faith, no matter how small, Jesus can help lead us to healing. He welcomes all, so make a friend, be a friend, and bring a friend to Christ. He welcomes friends old and new with forgiveness and open arms.

Use with *Jesus and the Lame Man* (page 94). Cut a hole in top of shoebox for the lame man and his friends. Use the circle of puppets on pages 87 and 88 as the crowd surrounding Jesus. Use removable adhesive to place them around Jesus in the room. Glue the lame man and his friends to a craft stick. Attach the Scribes to the shoebox with removable adhesive. Glue the healed man to a craft stick.

Jesus

Use with *Jesus and the Lame Man* (page 94). Copy, color, cut out, and glue the doors, windows, and furniture to a shoebox as shown on page 94.

The Demon-Possessed Man
Luke 8:26-39

Jesus and His disciples
sailed across a lake.
There they met a man
whom demons wanted to take.

Jesus and disciples appear.

Demon-possessed man appears.

He didn't have a house
and his body was bare.
Demons lived inside him;
they went with him everywhere.

But Jesus sent the demons
into a herd of swine.
They rushed out of the man.
Now, the man was fine!

Jesus faces the herd of pigs.

Then the pigs went running.
Down a steep bank they did go.
Those pigs with demons
drowned in the lake below.

Pig runs to the top of the hill and falls into the water.

Those who were caring for the pigs
couldn't believe their eyes.
They went through town and country
telling the big surprise.

Caretakers appear.

Caretakers walk around the shoebox.

People came to see
how the demons had been beat.
There they saw the man
sitting dressed at Jesus' feet.

Formerly demon-possessed man sits at the feet of Jesus.

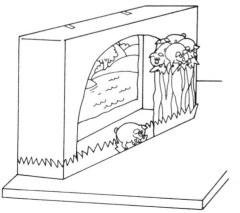

Questions
1. Where did Jesus put the demons?
2. What happened to the pigs?
3. What happened to the man?

Lesson
People are made in the image of God. Sometimes, like the demon-possessed man, people have thoughts and feelings—like jealousy—that take them away from God. Everyone sins, but through faith in Christ Jesus everyone is also a child of God. When you have feelings inside you that hurt your relationship with God or your neighbor, Jesus will help you heal. When you repent, or turn away from sinful thoughts and ways back toward God, you are forgiven and are on the way to healing.

Use with *The Demon-Possessed Man* (page 97). Use removable adhesive to attach the pig to the center of the shoebox as shown on page 97.

Jesus

Caretakers

Demon-possessed man

Use with *The Demon-Possessed Man* (page 97). Copy, color, and cut out the pigs and grass below. Attach the grass to the front of the shoebox. Attach the herd of pigs to the stage during the poem as shown on page 97.

Use with *The Demon-Possessed Man* (page 97). Use removable adhesive to attach the scene below to the back of the shoebox as shown on page 97.

The Loaves and the Fish
Mark 6

Lots of people everywhere
followed Jesus every day!
Jesus and the disciples
needed to get away.

Crowds appear.
Jesus appears.
Disciples appear.

Jesus said, "Come with me
to a quiet place to rest.
A break from all this crowd
I think would be the best."

Jesus and disciples walk.

But when they came together
at their very special place,
there were already people there
meeting Jesus face to face.

Crowd meets them.

The disciples told Jesus
to send these people away.
They couldn't possibly feed them all.
The disciples thought there was no way!

Disciples face Jesus.

"How many loaves do you have?" asked Jesus.
"Please just go and see."
"Five loaves of bread
and only two fish—no, not even three!"

Disciples move away.

Food appears on the table.

Jesus took the loaves and fish,
thanked God, and looked to heaven.
The loaves and fish grew to many more,
many more, that is, than seven!

Jesus holds loaf and fish.
Jesus looks up.
All baskets appear.
Food appears in baskets.

Jesus fed them one and all—
people, people, galore!
Five thousand people ate and ate
until they could eat no more.

Jesus feeds the people.

Questions
1. How many loaves did the disciples have at the beginning?
2. How many fish did they have?
3. Did the disciples want to feed the people?
4. What did Jesus do before the loaves and fish grew in number?
5. How many people ate?

Lesson
The size of the crowd following Jesus was huge. Although the disciples wanted to send them away, Jesus knew he could provide for the people's hunger. He gave thanks, broke the bread, and shared it. There was more than enough food for the five thousand; not only was everyone full, but there were leftovers! Sometimes we are hungry for God. When we go to God to get to know Him better, He will fill us.

Use with *The Loaves and the Fish* (page 101). Use removable adhesive to attach the loaves and the fish to the table. Make two copies of the disciples and glue one above the other on a jumbo craft stick to make twelve disciples.

Jesus

Use with *The Loaves and the Fish* (page 101). Color the baskets and cut them out as one large piece to attach to the foreground as shown on page 101. Attach the crowd to the shoebox as well.

Use with *The Loaves and the Fish* (page 101). Copy, color, cut out, and glue the mountains to the shoebox as shown on page 101.

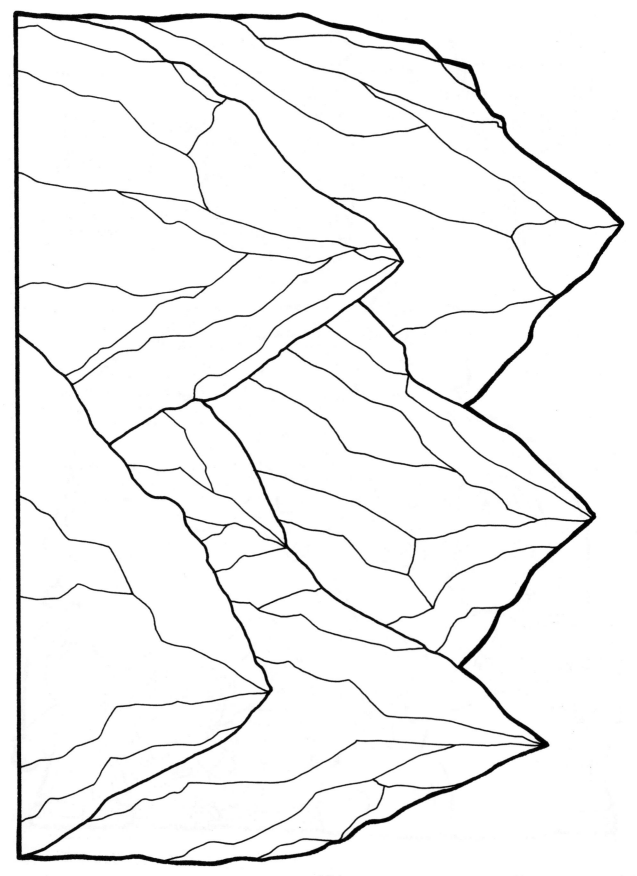

       Bible Story Puppets and Poems

Jesus told the disciples
to get into a boat.
They cast it out upon the lake,
and there they were afloat.

Jesus appears.

*Disciples get into the boat.
Boat leans sideways.*

Jesus didn't go with them.
He stayed on the mountain to pray.
But when he decided to meet them,
he went without delay.

Jesus goes to the mountain.

He stepped on the surface of the sea
and the disciples cried out for fear.
Jesus told them who was on the water
and said, "Be of good cheer."

He moves toward the disciples.

Jesus tried to calm them
and told them what to do.
He told them to take courage.
"It is I" walking towards you.

Jesus walks on the water.

Then, Peter the disciple
across the water began to shout,
"Jesus, if it's really you,
ask me to come on out."

Peter speaks.

Jesus called to Peter
to meet Him on the sea.
Peter started walking
and his faith began to flee.

Jesus faces Peter.

Peter moves toward Jesus.

The blowing wind scared Peter,
and he began to think.
He took his eyes off Jesus,
and he began to sink!

*Peter looks away from Jesus.
Peter falls.*

Jesus quickly grabbed him
and scolded him for doubt.
The wind died down around them,
and the disciples began to shout.

Jesus pulls Peter up.

"Truly you are the Son of God.
That is what we feel."
Then, after the boat landed,
more people Jesus healed.

Everyone stands on the land.

Questions
1. Have you ever seen anyone walk on water?
2. Did Jesus walk on water?
3. Did Peter walk on water?
4. What happened to Peter?
5. What made the disciples think Jesus was the son of God?

Lesson
Jesus is all powerful, so it was easy for Him to walk on water. Peter began walking on the surface until the wind scared him. Jesus was not just fully divine; He was fully human, too. He felt sad, angry, and joyful. He endured persecution in his own hometown and death on a cross for you and me. When you need to do things that are frightening but important, remember Jesus. Remember that you are not alone. It's okay to be scared, but Jesus likes it when we put Him, not fear, first.

Use with *Jesus Walks on Water* (page 105). Copy, color, cut out, and attach the waves to the shoebox as shown on page 105.

Jesus

Peter

Use with *Jesus Walks on Water* (page 105). Place the picture below between the mountains in the backgroud and the waves in the foreground as shown on page 105.

Use with *Jesus Walks on Water* (page 105). Glue the mountains to the back of the shoebox as shown on page 105.

A man went down from Jericho
and was resting on his way.
Some robbers stole his clothes,
beat him, and went away.

Injured man appears.

His clothes are taken.

Three men came along the road.
The first one was a cleric.
He passed on the other side
and perhaps thought the man barbaric.

Priest appears.

Priest walks far from him.

The next man was a Levite.
He acted just the same.
Finally, after more time passed,
a kind Samaritan came.

Levite appears.
Levite passes him by.

Samaritan appears.

He poured on oil and wine
and bandaged his wounds with care.
He placed him on his donkey;
The Samaritan was willing to share.

He puts on oil and wine and returns clothes to the injured man.
He puts the man on his donkey.
They move toward the inn.

They traveled on further
until they reached an inn.
He left money with the innkeeper
until he came again.

They stop at the inn.
Samaritan gives money to the innkeeper.

Which man loved his neighbor?
Oh, which one might it be?
It was the good Samaritan,
the person who showed mercy.

Priest, Levite, and Samaritan appear.

Samaritan moves forward.

Jesus says to be like the last man,
to show compassion for others
by doing like the Samaritan
and treating everyone as brothers.

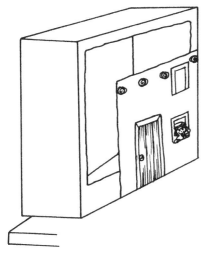

Questions
1. What happened to the man walking along the road?
2. How many people walked passed the man who was hurt?
3. Who finally helped him?
4. What things did the Samaritan do for the injured man?
5. Would you stop and help someone who was hurt or sad? Have you?

Lesson
In Bible times, Samaritan people were looked down upon. Other people thought they were better than Samaritans. When the man in this story was hurt, two people passed by. The Samaritan helped. He even left money to take care of the man. God is pleased when you show mercy like the Samaritan did.

Use with *The Good Samaritan* (page 109). Use removable adhesive to attach the coins to the innkeeper and the clothes and bandages to the injured man. Glue the donkey to a craft stick.

Injured Man

Priest

Levite

The Good Samaritan

Wine

OiL

Use with *The Good Samaritan* (page 109). Attach the picture below to the shoebox as shown on page 109.

Jesus loved Mary and Martha,
two sisters that he knew.
They had a brother, Lazarus,
and Jesus loved him, too.

Jesus, Mary, and Martha appear.

Lazarus appears.
All four stand together.

The sisters sent a message
to Jesus, "Lazarus is sick."
They hoped that Jesus would hurry
and come quick!

All except Jesus exit.
Jesus receives the message.

Jesus did not hurry.
He stayed gone two more days.
No one was sure why he did this.
It was just one of Jesus' ways.

Jesus moves slowly.

Before Jesus could get there
to be by Lazarus' side,
Lazarus took a turn for the worse,
and all at once he died.

Lazarus appears.

Lazarus dies.

When Jesus finally arrived,
the house was filled with gloom.
Lazarus already had been
four days in the tomb.

Jesus approaches the home.

Lazarus is in the tomb.

Martha said, "If you had been here,
my brother would not have died.
But I know that even now God will give you
whatever you ask," she sighed.

Martha speaks.

Then, Mary came and told him,
"Lord, if you had been here,
my brother would not have died."
Jesus heard this and shed many a tear.

Mary speaks.

Jesus weeps.

Jesus had men roll away the stone
and told Lazarus to come out.
Lazarus was alive again!
Jesus raised him up—no doubt!

Stone is moved.
Jesus looks at Lazarus.
Lazarus lives again.

Questions
1. What were the names of the sisters who were friends of Jesus?
2. Who became sick and died?
3. How did people feel about this?
4. What did Jesus do after Mary talked to him?
5. What did Jesus do to Lazarus?

Lesson
Lazarus was a very good friend of Jesus. Jesus was away when Lazarus died. Lazarus' sisters were upset that Jesus did not return sooner. They thought he could have healed Lazarus. Mary and Martha did not realize that Jesus had the power to bring him back to life. This story shows how Jesus cried for his friends. The story also reminds us of Jesus' great power to give people new life.

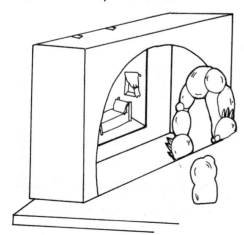

Bible Story Puppets and Poems

Use with *Jesus Raises Lazarus* (page 112). Use removable adhesive to attach Lazarus to the tomb and the note to Jesus' hand.

Lazarus

Jesus

Mary

Lazarus is sick

Copy tear from blue construction paper or color it with a blue marker. Attach to Jesus' face with removable adhesive.

Martha

Use with *Jesus Raises Lazarus* (page 112). Copy, color, cut out, and attach the room below to the back of the shoebox as shown on page 112.

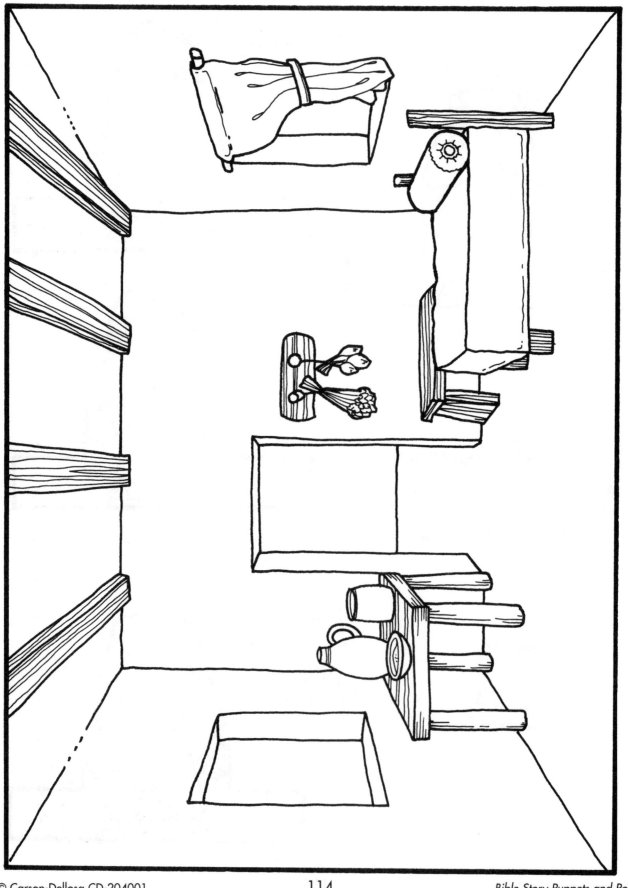

Use with *Jesus Raises Lazarus* (page 112). Copy, color, cut out, and attach the tomb to the front of the shoebox as shown on page 112.

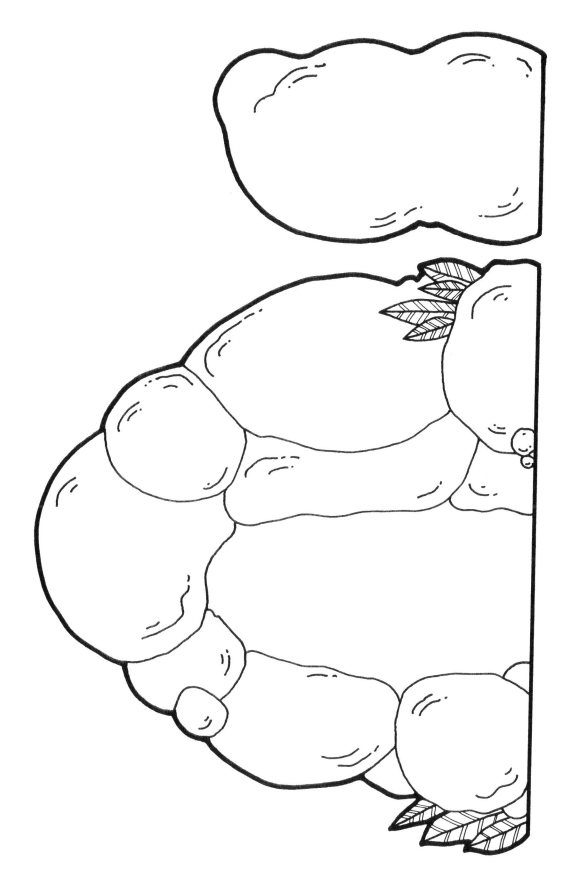

A sheep is missing.
Oh me, oh my!
He's missing—
oh what should I do?

Flock of sheep appear.

One sheep appears away from others.
Shepherd appears.

Keep on looking
and try to find him
or maybe
he will find you!

Shepherd looks for the stray sheep.

He's only one.
Oh me, oh my!
There still
are 99 more.

But he is
just as precious as the others.
He's the one
I'm searching for!

Help me find him
Oh me, oh my!
Help me
find him fast!

Shepherd looks at the audience.

I've found my sheep,
my precious sheep!
Rejoice with me.
He's found at last!

Shepherd finds the sheep.

Audience members clap.

We, too, are lost sheep,
oh me, oh my,
but Jesus forgives
our sin.

The rejoicing in heaven
when we repent
is like nothing you could ever
imagine.

Audience says, "Hallelujah!"

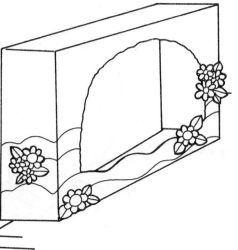

Questions
1. How many sheep did the shepherd have?
2. How many sheep did he lose?
3. Did he go looking for the one that was lost?
4. Did he find his lost sheep?
5. When he found it, what did he do?

Lesson
This lesson is not only about a shepherd who has lost one of his sheep. It is also about Jesus, the good shepherd. People are like sheep. Sometimes they follow the voice of their shepherd and other times they stray. Jesus never gives up on his people. If any one person is lost, he will search for and find her. Staying close to Jesus and obeying his Word helps us stay close to God and each other. If you lose your way, Jesus, the good shepherd, will find you and rejoice!

Use with *The Lost Sheep* (page 116). Use removable adhesive to attach the flock of sheep to the shoebox or glue the flock to a craft stick. Copy as many flowers as desired to decorate the shoebox as shown on page 116.

Jesus/Shepherd

Lost Sheep

There was a man who had two sons
and had a large estate.
The younger son asked for his share.
He didn't want to wait.

Father and sons appear.
Father holds the money.

Younger son speaks to his dad.

The father kindly gave it
although he was filled with doubt.
The younger son took it
and for a distant country set out.

Father gives him money.

Only the younger son leaves.

The son enjoyed wild living
and spent every penny.
Food became hard to find.
The son could not find any!

His money disappears.

He soon became so hungry
he longed for the food of a pig.
But no one gave him anything,
not even a single fig!

He looks at the pig.

Pig disappears.

The son finally woke up.
He came to his senses.
He could work on his father's farm,
have money for food and expenses.

Younger son tilts his head.

He decided he would go home
and tell his troubles to his dad.
He'd tell him he was sorry
and tell him he'd been bad.

He walks toward the mountain.

But while the son was still
quite far from home,
the father ran and kissed him
hoping never more he'd roam.

Father runs to meet him.

His dad said, "Bring a robe and sandals
and for his finger, bring a ring."
His father was glad to have him back.
He'd give him anything!

Father gives him a robe and sandals.
Father gives him a ring.

Bring the fattened calf and kill it.
We will have a feast; gather around!
This son of mine once was lost,
but now he has been found!

Fattened calf appears.

Guests arrive for the feast.

Questions
1. Who wanted his money from his father?
2. What did he do with his money?
3. What did he have to eat after he spent all his money?
4. Where did he decide to go next?
5. Was his father angry with him?

Lesson
The Lost Son is about how people stray from their father God. They may go far away from Him and do foolish things. When things don't go well, they return to God and ask His forgiveness. God is like the father in this story. He does not stay angry with His children. He forgives them because He loves them. If you do something wrong, ask God for forgiveness. He will be waiting with open arms to forgive you—just like the father in the story.

Use with *The Lost Son* (page 118). Glue the pig and the calf to craft sticks. Use removable adhesive to attach money to the father's and younger son's hands.

Father

Older Son

Younger Son

Use with *The Lost Son* (page 118). Use removable adhesive to attach the robe, sandals, and the ring to the younger son. Glue each set of party guests to a craft stick. Copy, color, cut out, and attach the mountains to the shoebox as shown on page 118.

"Good teacher," a rich young man asked,
"How do I get eternal life?"
"No one is good except God alone.
Obey the commandments. Love your wife!"

Rich young man faces Jesus.

Jesus speaks.

"Teacher, I have been good
since I was just a boy.
Tell me just this one thing,
and I'll be filled with joy."

Rich young man speaks.

"Go, sell what you have.
Give to the poor.
The treasures you will have in heaven
mean so much more."

Jesus responds.
Coins appear.

The rich young man became sad.
He didn't like this advice.
This seemed to him
a very costly price!

Rich young man's face has a frown.

Dollar signs appear.

The disciples then asked Jesus,
"Who then can enter in?"
He said, "With God it's possible.
With God, everyone can win!"

Disciples face Jesus.

Jesus speaks.

Jesus then spoke to them.
To truth he would attest.
"All those who follow after me
will be forever blessed!"

Disciples' hearts are visible.

Questions
1. What is eternal life?
2. Who wanted to know how to get it?
3. What did Jesus tell him to do?
4. Why did the young man become sad?
5. Who should the young man follow to get eternal life?

Lesson
The rich young man thought he could earn eternal life by being good. Jesus wanted him to see that no one is really good except God. Jesus told him to sell everything and give to the poor. The young man became sad because he did not want to lose his Earthly riches. Jesus wanted the young man to obey what he said and to leave material things for a different kind of treasure. God is pleased when we share what we have with others and are led by His Word and the example of His Son rather than by money.

Use with *The Rich Young Man* (page 121). Use removable adhesive to attach the dollar signs and changed face to the young man, coins to the shoebox, and the hearts to the disciples. Attach the disciples to a craft stick.

Rich Young Man

Jesus

Use with *The Rich Young Man* (page 121). Copy, color, cut out, and attach the Temple to the shoebox as shown on page 121.

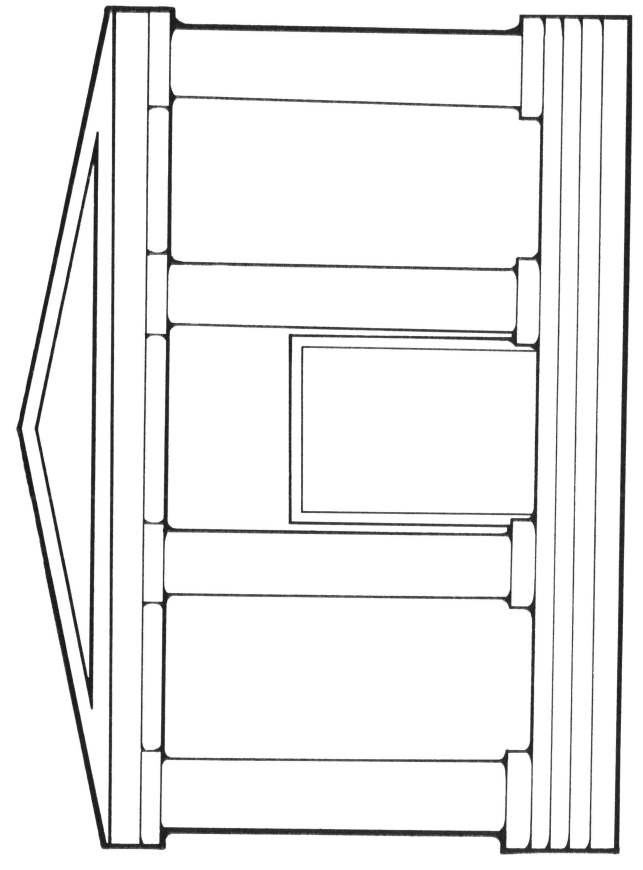

In Jericho Jesus was
just passing through.   *Jesus walks.*
Some people crowded in to see him,
and a man named Zacchaeus did, too. *Zacchaeus appears.*

Zacchaeus collected taxes   *Money bag appears.*
and he was also rich,   *Treasure chest and jewels appear.*
but when he tried to see Jesus,
there was just one hitch.   *Zacchaeus jumps up to see Jesus.*

Zacchaeus had a problem.
He wasn't very tall.
In fact, most people in Jericho
thought that he was small.

Zacchaeus got an idea
and though he was very wee,
he ran ahead on down the street   *Zacchaeus runs.*
and shimmied up a tree!   *Zacchaeus sits in the tree.*

When Jesus came, he told him   *Jesus looks at him.*
to come down right away,
because it was important
Jesus stay at his house that day.

The people started talking
because they thought Zacchaeus was bad,
but Zacchaeus surprised them
and shared the riches he had.   *He shares chocolate gold coins.*

Zacchaeus learned a lesson that day
about how he should behave
because Jesus the Son of Man had come
to seek and to save.   *Jesus stands next to Zacchaeus.*

Questions

1. What size man was Zacchaeus?
2. What kind of job did Zacchaeus have?
3. Who did Zacchaeus want to see?
4. How did Zacchaeus get to see Jesus?
5. What did Zacchaeus share after Jesus stayed at his house?

Lesson

In Bible times, many tax collectors took money that was not theirs. Zacchaeus, a tax collector, loved Jesus. When people grumbled about Jesus going to his house, he said to Jesus, "Look, Lord! Here and now I give half of my possessions to the poor, and if I have cheated anybody out of anything, I will pay back four times the amount." (Luke 19:8) Jesus did not see Zacchaeus just as a tax collector. He saw him as "a son of Abraham" (Luke 19:9). God is pleased when we see the good instead of assume the worst in others.

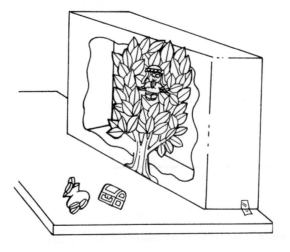

Use with *Zacchaeus Tries to See Jesus* (page 124). Attach sitting Zacchaeus with removable adhesive to the top of the tree. Attach the money bag, treasure chest, and jewels to the shoebox at the bottom of the tree.

Jesus

Zacchaeus

Use with *Zacchaeus Tries to See Jesus* (page 124). Copy, color, cut out, and attach the tree below to the shoebox as shown on page 124.

There once was a zealot.
The people called him Saul.
He did not like Christians.
He tormented them one and all.

Saul kept living
in darkness and deception
until one day the Lord Jesus
wanted to make a connection.

Jesus appeared to Saul
in a flash of bright light.
God's goodness was so great
that Saul lost his sight!

For three days straight,
nothing could Saul see
until Ananias healed him
and Jesus set him free.

It was in that instant
the scales from his eyes fell.
From then on, he would try
to treat all Christians well.

No longer would we hear
of Christians hurt by Saul.
Jesus changed his life
and called him Apostle Paul.

Saul appears.

Christians appear.
Saul chases Christians.

Christians hide.
Jesus appears.

He moves closer to Saul.
Flashlight shines.

Saul has blindfold.

Jesus exits. Saul is alone.

Ananias appears.
Jesus appears.

Scales fall.

Saul talks to the Christians.

Saul stands by Jesus.
They bow.

Questions
1. What did Saul think of Christians?
2. Did Jesus like the way Saul acted?
3. Why did Jesus appear to Saul?
4. Did Saul stay blind?
5. How did Saul treat people after he was blind and had met Jesus?

Lesson
Saul wanted to imprison Christians. He made murderous threats against them. Saul changed his mind about Jesus once he met him. Jesus became real to him. When Saul asked, "Who are you, Lord?" Jesus replied, "I am Jesus, whom you are persecuting" (Acts 9: 5-6). Saul knew he must leave his old life of persecuting Christians and begin preaching the good news of Jesus. When we hurt others, we hurt Jesus. God is pleased when we, like Paul, change our lives. God is pleased when we respond with love to people who are persecuted today.

Use with *Saul Becomes Blind* (page 127). Cut out the scales, glue them to the rectangular piece below, and attach the "blindfold" to a small craft stick. Then lay the stick down when the scales fall from Paul's eyes. Glue the group of Christians to a craft stick. Draw a road and rocks along the bottom of a shoebox as shown on page 127.

Saul/Paul

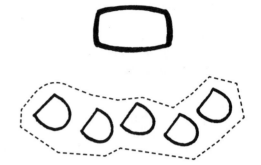

Ananias

Jesus